I Have Been Born Again,

What Next?

by

Charles Brock

Published by
Church Growth International
13174 Owens Lane
Neosho, Missouri, 64850

Copyright by Charles Brock

ISBN: 1-885504-15-2

CONTENTS

Suggested Use of These Lessons

1. After members of a Bible Study group are born again, they may wish to continue in their group Bible studies. This book is designed to be used by these groups. The lessons can be used to prepare a group of new Christians to become a church.

2. A church may use this book for new-member classes.

A Suggested Way to Study These Lessons

1. Study one lesson each week.

2. Allow one hour for each lesson.

3. Permit class members to participate in reading, either by paragraphs or pages. For the review and discussion period, let class members read the questions and search for the answers. The answers are found in the lesson.

Introduction

These lessons are written to help the believer in his new life as a born-again Christian. The theme of the lessons is found in 2 Corinthians 5:17: *When anyone is joined to Christ, he is a new being; the old is gone, the new has come.*

The 11 lessons deal with basic elements found in the new life of the believer:

* A New Nature
* A New Power: the Holy Spirit
* A New Guide: Bible Study
* A New Privilege: Prayer
* A New Hope
* New Relationships
* A New Understanding of Baptism
* A New Family: the Church
* A New Reminder: the Lord's Supper
* A New Opportunity: Tithing
* New Responsibilities

When a person is born again, it is just the beginning of a new life. A study of these lessons will help the believer get started in successfully living the new life.

It is important to note that these lessons are relevant topics wrapped in Scripture. The Bible is the authority, therefore Scripture is used extensively. Some class members will want to follow the Scripture reading in their Bibles while others may prefer to follow the Scripture reading that is printed in the lessons. The Scripture is printed in the lessons because it allows the class members to share the same translation and for the convenience of those new believers who may not have a Bible.

Scripture quotations are from *Today's English Version.* The author has used bold print for emphasis in some of the Scripture.

LESSON ONE

A NEW NATURE

When anyone is joined to Christ, he is a new being; the old is gone, the new has come. 2 Corinthians 5:17

When a person is born again, he has a new nature. There is a great change in his attitudes and actions.

This new life or new nature became ours when we confessed our sinful condition to Christ and turned from sin to place full faith in him. New life was the free gift to us from God. This is the meaning of being born again.

In Romans 6:23 we read, *For sin pays its wage—death; but God's free gift is eternal life in union with Christ Jesus our Lord.*

IN THIS LESSON WE WILL STUDY ABOUT OUR NEW LIFE AND NEW NATURE.

The Bible describes the old nature and the new nature. The old nature was our life before we were born again. The new nature is our life after we are born again.

These two natures are clearly seen in Galatians 5:19-26. In these verses Paul describes the fruits and results of the two natures.

What human nature does is quite plain. It shows itself in immoral, filthy, and indecent actions; in worship of idols and witchcraft.

6

People become enemies and they fight; they become jealous, angry, and ambitious. They separate into parties and groups; they are envious, get drunk, have orgies, and do other things like these. I warn you now as I have before: those who do these things will not possess the Kingdom of God. Galatians 5:19-21

But the Spirit produces love, joy, peace, patience, kindness, goodness, faithfulness, humility, and self-control. There is no law against such things as these. And those who belong to Christ Jesus have put to death their human nature with all its passions and desires. The Spirit has given us life; he must also control our lives. We must not be proud or irritate one another or be jealous of one another. Galatians 5:22-26

The Fruit of the Old Nature

From Galatians 5:19-21, list some of the sins found in the old nature.

Remember, this is a description of human nature without Christ as Savior and Lord.

The Fruit of the New Nature

Paul describes the new nature in Galatians 5:22-26. Read these verses again. There are nine new things found in the new life. They are produced by the Holy Spirit living in our lives. Please list these new characteristics.

Note verse 25: *The Spirit has given us life; he must also control our lives.*

Read again 2 Corinthians 5:17, found at the beginning of this lesson.

Paul says in Ephesians 4:22-24: *So get rid of your old self, which made you live as you used to--the old self that was being destroyed by its deceitful desires. Your hearts and minds must be made completely new, and you must put on the new self, which is created in God's likeness and reveals itself in the true life that is upright and holy.*

For additional study on the old life and the new life, read Colossians 3:5-17.

We have seen from the Bible that the new life is normal for the believer. We also understand that the true believer cannot live like he did before he was born again. The new life replaces the old life.

The believer has new attitudes and new actions.

You may say: "I have been born again. My life has really changed, but sometimes I am tempted to sin, and sometimes I do sin. Am I still a born-again Christian?"

Some new Christians become very frustrated and depressed when they receive Christ one day as Savior and Lord and the next day they sin.

Is this normal? Am I the only one like this? Do I lose my salvation? Many people ask these questions.

So that we may understand ourselves and the way we act, we will study more closely the believer's relationship to temptation and sin.

THE BORN-AGAIN CHRISTIAN IS FREE FROM *SLAVERY* TO SIN BECAUSE OF TWO FACTS.

1. The believer **has received a new nature as a gift from God.**

1 John 3:9-10: *Whoever is a child of God does not continue to sin, for God's very nature is in him, and because God is his Father, he cannot continue to sin. Here is the clear difference between God's children and the Devil's children: anyone who does not do what is right or does not love his brother is not God's child.*

You will notice the words in verse 9 above, "cannot continue to sin." This does not mean that a believer cannot sin. Every believer sins. But the emphasis is on "continue" or continuously. The Christian will not be a slave to sin. He will not habitually live a life of sin. The new nature will bring new fruits.

2. The new believer is free from slavery to sin because **he has the Holy Spirit living in his life.**

1 John 4:13: *We are sure that we live in union with God and that he lives in union with us, because he has given us his Spirit.*

1 John 4:4: *But you belong to God, my children, and have defeated the false prophets, because the Spirit who is in you is more powerful than the spirit in those who belong to the world.*

Therefore, from the Bible we see that a born-again Christian does not continuously live in sin because God gives the Christian **a new nature** and **the Holy Spirit.** The Holy Spirit becomes our daily companion when we believe and receive Christ as Savior and Lord.

Conclusion: sin no longer dominates our lives because we have a new godly nature and we have a new director of our lives, the Holy Spirit of God.

We know that we have a new nature and the Holy Spirit living within us because our attitudes and actions change.

If a person claims to be born again but continues to enjoy the old sinful life, he is not really born again.

Now back to the question, will a born-again Christian sin? The answer is yes.

Another question: Will a born-again Christian habitually enjoy living in sin? The answer is no.

Sin **dominates** and lives comfortably in the life of the unbeliever.

For the believer, sin is an **intruder** that does not belong. The believer is not comfortable with the presence of sin.

When a person is born again, there is a new awareness of sin. There is a new sin-sensitive conscience.

Does the believer become lost and condemned when he sins? No, he does not. He will be unhappy, and if the sin is not confessed to God, the believer may lose some of the joy of his salvation. But once a person is God's child with eternal life, nothing can separate him from God.

Romans 8:39: *...there is nothing in all creation that will ever be able to separate us from the love of God which is ours through Christ Jesus our Lord.*

WHAT DOES THE BELIEVER DO WHEN HE SINS?

John says: *If we say that we have no sin, we deceive ourselves, and there is no truth in us. But if we confess our sins to God, he will keep his promise and do what is right: he will forgive us our sins and purify us from all our wrongdoing.* 1 John 1:8-9

Also in 1 John 2:1-2: *I am writing this to you, my children, so that you will not sin; but if anyone does sin, we have someone who pleads with the Father on our behalf—Jesus Christ, the righteous one. And Christ himself is the means by which our sins are forgiven, and not our sins only, but also the sins of everyone.*

When a believer sins, he immediately confesses that sin directly to God and asks forgiveness. God forgives the sin, and the believer is cleansed from the sin.

WHAT ABOUT TEMPTATION?

Jesus Christ was tempted.

Matthew 4:1: *Then the Spirit led Jesus into the desert to be tempted by the Devil.*

Hebrews 2:18: *And now he can help those who are tempted, because he himself was tempted and suffered.*

Hebrews 4:15: *...we have a High Priest who was tempted in every way that we are, but did not sin.*

Christ was tempted, but he did not sin. It is not a sin to be tempted. To give in to temptation is sin.

Jesus said to his disciples, ...*keep watch, and pray that you will not fall into temptation.* Mark 14:38

To be tempted is not a sin, but to allow ourselves to be in a position where temptation is constant is unhealthy and dangerous. We should avoid temptation as much as possible.

FOR REVIEW AND DISCUSSION

1. The Bible tells of two natures. One is the old nature and the other is the _____ _____.

2. Name some of the things seen in the old nature. Galatians 5:19-21

3. Describe the new nature. Galatians 5:22-26

4. In this lesson we learned that the believer is free from slavery to sin because he has received a ____ _____ from God and because he has the _____ _____ living in his life.

5. When does the believer receive the Holy Spirit? Acts 11:17

6. Will a true Christian commit sin? Yes ___ No ___

7. According to this lesson, what is the Christian to do when he sins? 1 John 1:9

8. The born-again Christian will have new attitudes and new actions in his life. True ___ False ___

9. How has your life changed since you were born again?

10. Is it a sin to be tempted? Yes ___ No ___
    In what ways are you tempted?

11. How can a believer overcome temptation?

A NEW POWER: THE HOLY SPIRIT

After a person is born again he faces a new direction in life. Things change at home in the family. There is a change in relationships at work. There is a new reason for living. It is a new and exciting life. There are new challenges. There are new problems. There are new temptations. **There is a new power to assist in living the new life.** This new power is the Holy Spirit. *For the Spirit that God has given us does not make us timid; instead, his Spirit fills us with power, love, and self-control.* 2 Timothy 1:7

In this lesson we will answer the following questions:
Who is the Holy Spirit?
How does a person receive the Holy Spirit?
When does a person receive the Holy Spirit?
How can I know I have the Holy Spirit?
How does the Holy Spirit help the believer?

WHO IS THE HOLY SPIRIT?

When Jesus was nearing the end of his earthly life, he spoke to his followers about hope and victory for the days ahead. Hope and victory would not be found in their own strength. Jesus said even as he had been with them, **he would send another like himself to dwell within them.** Read the words of Jesus as recorded in the book of John.

"...Whoever loves me will obey my teaching. My Father will love him, and my Father and I will come to him and live with him.

15

Whoever does not love me does not obey my teaching. And the teaching you have heard is not mine, but comes from the Father, who sent me. I have told you this while I am still with you. The Helper, the Holy Spirit, whom the Father will send in my name, will teach you everything and make you remember all that I have told you." John 14:23-26

Again we read the words of Jesus: *"The Helper will come—the Spirit, who reveals the truth about God and who comes from the Father. I will send him to you from the Father, and he will speak about me..."* John 15:26-27

After the resurrection of Jesus he gave the following command to his followers: *"Go, then, to all peoples everywhere and make them my disciples: baptize them in the name of the Father, the Son, and the Holy Spirit, and teach them to obey everything I have commanded you. And I will be with you always, to the end of the age."* Matthew 28:19-20

After Jesus was resurrected he appeared to many different groups. There was no doubt he did what no other had done. He died and after three days in the grave came forth never to die again.

Let us listen to what the Bible says about this in Acts 1:3-11: *For forty days after his death he appeared to them many times in ways that proved beyond doubt that he was alive. They saw him, and he talked with them about the Kingdom of God. And when they came together, he gave them this order: "Do not leave Jerusalem, but wait for the gift I told you about, the gift my Father promised. John baptized with water, but in a few days you will be baptized with the Holy Spirit." When the apostles met together with Jesus, they asked Him, "Lord, will you at this time give the Kingdom back to Israel?" Jesus said to them, "The times and occasions are set by my Father's own authority, and it is not for you to know when they will be. But when the Holy Spirit comes upon you, you will be filled*

16

with power, and you will be witnesses for me in Jerusalem, in all of Judea and Samaria, and to the ends of the earth." After saying this, he was taken up to heaven as they watched him, and a cloud hid him from their sight.

This was the beginning of a great movement called Christianity. The book of Acts in the New Testament is a story of how people came to know Jesus as their personal Savior and Lord. But it does not stop there. It is a story of how these people received new power to face life victoriously. It is a story of how the Holy Spirit came to live in the lives of these believers to empower them to be witnesses of Jesus.

Who is the Holy Spirit?

1. He is a part of the trinity.

There is God the Father, Jesus the Son, and the Holy Spirit. With our limited human wisdom we do not understand the trinity, but the Bible declares this to be a fact. They are three yet one. By faith we accept this. We will be blessed if we just accept it and don't try to speculate about how it can be.

2. The Holy Spirit is a person just as Jesus is a person. We do not refer to the Holy Spirit as an "it." He is personal.

3. The Holy Spirit was the One to indwell the hearts of all believers after Jesus went back to his Father after the resurrection.

4. He is God's gift to those who receive his Son Jesus as Savior and Lord.

The Holy Spirit is the personal presence of God in the life of every true believer.

HOW DOES A PERSON RECEIVE THE HOLY SPIRIT?

The Bible says, *Peter said to them, "Each one of you must turn away from his sins and be baptized in the name of Jesus Christ, so that your sins will be forgiven; and you will receive God's gift, the Holy Spirit."* Acts 2:38

In Acts 5:32 we read, *"We are witnesses to these things—we and the Holy Spirit, who is God's **gift to** those who obey him."*

The Holy Spirit is not deserved or earned, but he is God's gift to every believer.

WHEN DOES A PERSON RECEIVE THE HOLY SPIRIT?

The Bible says, *It is clear that God gave those Gentiles the same gift that he gave us **when we believed in the Lord Jesus Christ;**....* Acts 11:17

Acts 10:47: *These people have received the Holy Spirit, just as we also did. Can anyone, then, stop them from being baptized with water?*

According to these verses, one receives the Holy Spirit when he receives Jesus. Everyone who has received Christ as Savior and Lord received at the same time the presence of the Holy Spirit. There is no waiting period after a person is saved. When he is saved, he also receives the Holy Spirit. The Holy Spirit does not leave the believer. The believer may grieve the Holy Spirit by drifting away from God's will, but the Holy Spirit does not go away or forsake the believer no matter what the conditions may be.

18

HOW DO WE KNOW WE HAVE THE HOLY SPIRIT IN OUR LIVES?

The promises of the Bible, God's Holy Word, are true and can be believed. The following verses are just some of many telling us of the presence of the Holy Spirit in the believer's life.

Paul said: *Don't you know that your body is the temple of the Holy Spirit, who lives in you and who was given to you by God? You do not belong to yourselves but to God; He bought you for a price. So use your bodies for God's glory.* 1 Corinthians 6:19-20

When the Holy Spirit lives in a person's life, his presence is obvious. We can know and feel his presence. We sense there has been a beautiful addition to our lives that makes a difference in all we do.

The Bible says, "*...it is God himself who has set us apart, who has given us the Holy Spirit in our hearts as the guarantee of all that he has in store for us.*" 2 Corinthians 1:21b, 22b

There is an obvious change in the life of a person who has been saved. If there is no change, there is no new life. In some the change is more dramatically seen than in others, but there will be change. The Bible says: *When anyone is joined to Christ, he is a new being; the old is gone, the new has come. All this is done by God, who through Christ changed us from enemies into his friends and gave us the task of making others his friends also.* 2 Corinthians 5:17-18

The change does not stop after we are saved. It continues as maturity is experienced. The Bible says, *At one time you yourselves used to live according to such desires, when your life was dominated by them. But now you must get rid of all these things: anger, passion, and hateful feelings. No insults or obscene talk*

19

must ever come from your lips. Do not lie to one another, for you have put off the old self with its habits and have put on the new self. This is the new being which God, its Creator, is constantly renewing in his own image, in order to bring you to a full knowledge of himself. Colossians 3:7-10

How do we know we have the Holy Spirit in our lives? <u>We will see a difference that cannot be brought about by our own strength.</u> We see a sustained new life that grows in love for God and for others that cannot be the result of human strength alone. There is **observable fruit.** In Galatians 5:22-26 we see a list of the new qualities seen in the life of the believer, qualities that are the result of the Holy Spirit's presence. You may want to refer to these verses on page 7 in lesson one.

HOW DOES THE HOLY SPIRIT HELP THE BELIEVER?

1. <u>He produces a new nature.</u> The new believer has new attitudes and actions, as seen in Colossians 3:7-10 above and Galatians 5:22-26 on page 7.

2. <u>The believer receives strength and ability to serve.</u> When a person is saved, he becomes a part of God's Kingdom. Others who have accepted Christ are also a part of that Kingdom. All these people combined form a family called the church. In this family relationship every member of the body is of great importance. God gives each member a very important responsibility. But this responsiblity/service is not carried out in human strength alone.

The Bible says: *There are different kinds of spiritual gifts, but the same Spirit gives them. There are different ways of serving, but the same Lord is served. There are different abilities to perform service, but the same God gives ability to everyone for their particular service. The Spirit's presence is shown in some way in each person for the good of all.* I Corinthians 12:4-7

20

3. The Holy Spirit enables the believer to unashamedly confess Jesus as Lord of life. I Corinthians 12:3b, ...*no one can confess "Jesus is Lord," unless he is guided by the Holy Spirit.* When a person accepts Jesus as Savior and Lord, there will be a desire to share the good news.

4. The Holy Spirit brings understanding.
So then, we do not speak in words taught by human wisdom, but in words taught by the Spirit, as we explain spiritual truths to those who have the Spirit. Whoever does not have the Spirit cannot receive the gifts that come from God's Spirit. Such a person really does not understand them; they are nonsense to him, because their value can be judged only on a spiritual basis.
1 Corinthians 2:13-14

The believer has a new understanding of the things of God. He will have clearer understanding of the Bible. This helps us see why an unbeliever cannot understand the Bible. God's Word will not mean much to a person until he has been born again, for it is then that he has the Holy Spirit to bring enlightenment.

5. The Holy Spirit becomes the teacher for the believer.
Jesus said: *"I have told you this while I am still with you. The Helper, the Holy Spirit, whom the Father will send in my name, will teach you everything and make you remember all that I have told you."* John 14:25-26

But as for you, Christ has poured out his Spirit on you. As long as his Spirit remains in you, you do not need to have anyone to teach you. For his Spirit teaches you about everything, and what he teaches is true, not false. Obey the Spirit's teaching, then, and remain in union with Christ. I John 2:27

So wherever in the world a believer lives, he is not alone. He has the best teacher and leader in the world, the Holy Spirit of God. The

21

believer may live among many believers where there are many church leaders, but the Holy Spirit is still the primary teacher. If the believer lives in a part of the world where there are few believers and no Christian leaders, can he survive? Who will he turn to? It is important to remember he is never alone. As long as he lives, he will have the Holy Spirit to guide him and teach him in all things. It is important to remember the Holy Spirit leads a person primarily as the Bible is studied. So every believer must daily read the Bible and ask the Holy Spirit to show him the truth.

6. The Holy Spirit will lead the believer to victory over Satan and the evil spirits of this world.

Witchcraft and evil spirits will no longer have power to control the believer. It is normal for the new believer to encounter temptations from Satan. These temptations may be in the form of doubts about the genuineness of the conversion experience, they may be related to past habits and relationships. Continuing unwholesome activities or relationships will bring temptation. Through daily, prayerful Bible study, the Holy Spirit will help the believer to be victorious in each situation.

FOR REVIEW AND DISCUSSION

1. After his resurrection from the grave Jesus went back to his Father. The _Holy   Spirit_ was sent to comfort and lead the Christians.

2. In the trinity there is God the Father, Jesus the Son, and the _Holy Spirit_.

3. When does a believer receive the Holy Spirit?
   When he accept Christ

4. The Holy Spirit never leaves the believer. True _✓_ False___

5. In our lesson we learned six ways the Holy Spirit helps the believer? Please list these six.

23

A NEW GUIDE: BIBLE STUDY

There are many privileges to be enjoyed in the new life of a believer. In this lesson we will study about the privilege of Bible study.

WHY IS IT SO IMPORTANT TO READ THE BIBLE?

It is important to read the Bible because **the Bible is God's message to us**.

For no prophetic message ever came just from the will of man, but men were under the control of the Holy Spirit as they spoke the message that came from God. 2 Peter 1:21

The Bible is not an ordinary book. It is not man's word; it is God's Word. It is God speaking to us through men who were under his control. It is a personal message from God to you.

It is important to read the Bible because **it tells us about God**.

Since we are now God's children, we want to know as much as possible about our Father. From the beginning to the end, the Bible tells us who God is, how he works, and his purpose for man. To learn about God, we must read his book. It is exciting to learn from the Bible about his holiness, justice, mercy, and love. From the Bible we get an accurate picture of God as we read about Jesus Christ, his son. Jesus said, *Whoever has seen me has seen the Father.* John 14:9b

24

It is important to read the Bible because **it tells us about ourselves**.

In Genesis the Bible tells us that God created man and woman. In the New Testament Jesus tells us of the two possible destinations of each man and woman. The Bible reveals mankind as sinful and in need of the Savior. From the Bible we learn that the power sin has over us can be overcome through Jesus Christ.

It is important to read the Bible because **it tells us how to be successful in living the Christian life**.

But as for you, continue in the truths that you were taught and firmly believe. You know who your teachers were, and you remember that ever since you were a child, you have known the Holy Scriptures, which are able to give you the wisdom that leads to salvation through faith in Christ Jesus. All Scripture is inspired by God and is useful for teaching the truth, rebuking error, correcting faults, and giving instruction for right living, so that the person who serves God may be fully qualified and equipped to do every kind of good deed. 2 Timothy 3:14-17

According to these verses, all Scripture is inspired by God and is useful for _____, _____, _____, and _____.

From the verses above, we learn that it is possible for even a child to study and understand the Bible.

It is important to read the Bible because **it is food for the developing Christian**.

Jesus said, *"...man cannot live on bread alone, but needs every word that God speaks."* Matthew 4:4

For a person to be physically healthy, he needs food. For a Christian to be spiritually healthy, he must read and digest the Word of God.

HOW DO I READ THE BIBLE?

A systematic plan of Bible reading is necessary. Many people read their Bibles only when they feel a special urge. They open their Bibles and read a few verses or chapters wherever the Bible happens to open. This is haphazard rather than systematic. The person who is not systematic in his Bible reading usually will not be systematic in his time schedule of reading and will not read much from the Bible.

What is a systematic plan of Bible reading?

It may be best for the new believer to begin with Matthew, the first book of the New Testament, and read a certain number of chapters each day. After Matthew's Gospel has been read, continue by reading Mark's Gospel, the second book in the New Testament. In the 27 books of the New Testament, there is a total of 260 chapters. If you read two chapters each day, you will complete your reading of the New Testament in 19 weeks.

When you have read the entire New Testament, it would be good if you begin with Matthew and start through again. But also start reading from the Old Testament. Read two chapters from the Old Testament and one chapter from the New Testament each day. In the Old Testament begin with Genesis, the first book. If you read three chapters each day, you will read through the whole Bible in one year.

This is a systematic plan of Bible reading. Let this plan be your minimum reading. You will desire to make additional special studies of some parts of the Bible.

If you have only the Gospel of John, you should begin reading at least one chapter each day from it until you have read through it. If you still do not have a Bible, begin reading John's Gospel again. Plan to buy a Bible.

Some additional points on how to read the Bible:

1. Use a translation that is easy to understand.
2. Pray before you read. Thank God for his Word and ask him to help you understand what you read.
3. Be humble. It is God's Word, and it is inspired and powerful.
4. Underline words and verses that really catch your attention.

WHEN DO I READ THE BIBLE?

Just as you have decided to have a systematic plan for Bible reading, you also need a regular time to read.

This time will not be the same for everyone. For some, early morning is best, while others use the extra time at lunch break. For others, before going to bed may be best.

The important thing is to set your time and stay with it. An uncertain schedule often will mean no time for Bible study. Everyone is busy; therefore, a definite, regular time is necessary. Think about it; pray about it. Choose your time for Bible reading.

Begin to memorize verses.

Memorize as many verses as you can. When you find a great verse, write it down and keep it with you throughout the day, reading it often. When the day is over you will have memorized it.

In Psalm 119:11 we read, *I keep your law in my heart, so that I will not sin against you.*

Jesus said, "*...how happy are those who hear the Word of God and obey it.*" Luke 11:28

FOR REVIEW AND DISCUSSION

1. In this lesson we have studied a great privilege of the Christian. What is it?

2. List five reasons why it is important to read the Bible.

3. Discuss why a systematic plan of Bible reading is necessary.

4. You will read the entire New Testament in 19 weeks if you read _____ chapters daily.

5. Are you going to begin reading daily from your Bible? Yes _____
   No _____

6. If your answer is yes, where will you begin reading? _____
   How many chapters will you read each day? _____

7. At what time each day will you read the Bible? _____

8. Why is it important to memorize Bible verses?

LESSON 4

A NEW PRIVILEGE: PRAYER

We will now study another great privilege of the believer, the privilege of prayer. Four questions will be answered in this study.

What is prayer?
Why should I pray?
How do I pray?
When do I pray?

WHAT IS PRAYER?

Through the Bible, God talks to man. Through prayer, man talks to God. Prayer is communication with God. Prayer is spending time with God, talking to him and listening for his answer.

In Matthew 6:9, Jesus said, *This, then is how you should pray: Our Father in Heaven...*

Matthew 6:6: *But when you pray, go to your room, close the door, and pray to your Father, who is unseen. And your Father, who sees what you do in private, will reward you.*

These verses show that prayer is talking to **God**. Prayer is **not** talking to man.

When we were born again, God became our Father and we became his children. In John 1:12-13 we read: *Some, however, did receive him and believed in him; so he gave them the right to become*

God's children. They did not become God's children by natural means, that is, by being born as the children of a human father; God himself was their Father.

From these verses we find the basis for prayer. That basis is a Father-child relationship brought about by the new birth. Prayer is the privilege of the believer because of his new relationship with God as his Father. Prayer is a natural relationship of a father and child. Because God is our Father, we share with him our dreams, goals, problems, and praise. This is prayer.

WHY SHOULD I PRAY?

It is the natural thing to do. Our special relationship to God matures when we pray. God is our best and most trusted friend; therefore, we need to talk to him.

How do I thank God for daily blessings? Through prayer.
Be joyful always, pray at all times, be thankful in all circumstances. This is what God wants from you in your life in union with Christ Jesus. 1 Thessalonians 5:16-18

How do I receive forgiveness of sins? Through prayer.
But if we confess our sins to God, he will keep his promise and do what is right: he will forgive us our sins and purify us from all our wrongdoing. 1 John 1:9 A good example of prayer for forgiveness is found in Psalm 51.

How do I make my needs known to God? Through prayer.
Let us be brave, then, and approach God's throne, where there is grace. There we will receive mercy and find grace to help us just when we need it. Hebrews 4:16

But if any of you lacks wisdom, he should pray to God, who will give it to him; because God gives generously and graciously to all. James 1:5

Why should I pray?
Because it is natural for a child to talk to his Father.
Because I need to express my thankfulness to God.
Because I need forgiveness of sins.
Because I need to make my needs known to God.

Christ felt the need to pray. So must we.

HOW SHOULD I PRAY?

The disciples of Jesus said, ...*Lord, teach us to pray.* Luke 11:1

Before Jesus taught his disciples how to pray, he warned them against wrong ways to pray. He said, *"When you pray, do not be like the hypocrites! They love to stand up and pray in the houses of worship and on the street corners, so that everyone will see them. I assure you, they have already been paid in full.*

When you pray, do not use a lot of meaningless words, as the pagans do, who think that God will hear them because their prayers are long." Matthew 6:5, 7

Jesus continued speaking to his disciples about prayer. *"This, then, is how you should pray: 'Our Father in heaven: May your holy name be honored; may your Kingdom come; may your will be done on earth as it is in heaven. Give us today the food we need. Forgive us the wrongs we have done, as we forgive the wrongs that others have done to us. Do not bring us to hard testing, but keep us safe from the Evil One.' "* Matthew 6:9-13

This is called the Model Prayer. Jesus did not mean that believers should always repeat these exact words. When we read the prayers of Jesus and others in the New Testament, we see that they do not repeat these words. Jesus is saying that prayer includes praise and honor to God, obedience to the will of God, seeking God's help for daily needs such as food, confession of sin, and request for help in overcoming Satan, the Evil One. In our prayers we should be concerned about the same things found in the Model Prayer.

As a new believer, how should I learn to pray?

1. When you are alone, speak aloud to God.
2. You are not making a speech to God. Simply express your thoughts to him.
3. Remember your prayers are from your heart to God.
4. Pray with a family member or friend.
5. Pray every time before you eat, thanking God for his provisions.

WHEN DO I PRAY?

The new Christian should pray his first prayer immediately after he has been born again. That prayer may be something like this, "Jesus, thank you for saving me."

A grateful Christian will pray **before every meal**, expressing thanks.

It is best to **begin the day** with prayer, seeking God's guidance and protection throughout the day. At the **end of the day** or before sleeping, pray, thanking God for his guidance and protection throughout the day and for all other blessings.

This would establish a pattern of **five regular times** given to prayer every day. The believer will find it natural to pray spontaneously throughout the day, expressing thanks to God or asking for his help. You can pray as you walk, ride, etc.

A Christian must read the Bible and pray regularly if he is to be healthy spiritually. If you have a Bible, you may want to read some other verses about prayer:

Daniel 6:10
Matthew 18:20
Matthew 26:41
Luke 18:1
1 Thessalonians 5:17
Matthew 7:7
Mark 11:25
John 17

FOR REVIEW AND DISCUSSION

1. What is prayer?

2. We talk to _____ when we pray.

3. Why should the believer pray?

4. The prayer in Matthew 6:9-13 is called the _____ prayer.

5. From this lesson we have learned that the believer prays directly to God. True ___ False ___

6. Name five good times for the believer to pray.

A NEW HOPE

Before we were born again, we had no hope.

In Ephesians 2:12-14 Paul says: *At that time you were apart from Christ. You were foreigners and did not belong to God's chosen people. You had no part in the covenants, which were based on God's promises to his people, and you lived in this world without hope and without God. But now, in union with Christ Jesus you, who used to be far away, have been brought near by the sacrificial death of Christ. For Christ himself has brought us peace...*

A person who has not been born again lives without hope in this life. He also lives without hope of life in heaven.

But when a person has been born again, he has hope. We read about our new hope in 1 Peter 1:3-4: *Let us give thanks to the God and Father of our Lord Jesus Christ! Because of his great mercy he gave us new life by raising Jesus Christ from death. This fills us with a living hope, and so we look forward to possessing the rich blessings that God keeps for his people.*

The source of the new life and new hope is God. We must always remember to thank him for it.

NEW HOPE WHEN FACING DEATH

When we attend a funeral of a person who has not been born again and whose family has not been born again, it is clear that these people have **no hope**. For the believer it is different. Even when death comes, there **is hope**. Paul speaks of this in 1 Thessalonians.

I Thessalonians 4:13-18: *Our brothers, we want you to know the truth about those who have died, so that you will not be sad, as those who have no hope. We believe that Jesus died and rose again, and so we believe that God will take back with Jesus those who have died believing in him. What we are teaching you now is the Lord's teaching: we who are alive on the day the Lord comes will not go ahead of those who have died. There will be the shout of command, the archangel's voice, the sound of God's trumpet, and the Lord himself will come down from heaven. Those who have died believing in Christ will rise to life first; then we who are living at that time will be gathered up along with them in the clouds to meet the Lord in the air. And so we will always be with the Lord. So then, encourage one another with these words.*

Jesus told his disciples there is hope. *"Do not be worried and upset,"* Jesus told them. *"Believe in God and believe also in me. There are many rooms in my Father's house, and I am going to prepare a place for you. I would not tell you this if it were not so. And after I go and prepare a place for you, I will come back and take you to myself, so that you will be where I am."* John 14:1-3

Paul talks of our hope, of our resurrection, in 1 Corinthians 15:12-14, 17-20, below.

Now, since our message is that Christ has been raised from death, how can some of you say that the dead will not be raised to life? If that is true, it means that Christ was not raised; and if Christ has not been raised from death, then we have nothing to preach and you have nothing to believe.

37

And if Christ has not been raised, then your faith is a delusion and you are still lost in your sins. It would also mean that the believers in Christ who have died are lost. If our hope in Christ is good for this life only and no more, then we deserve more pity than anyone else in all the world. But the truth is that Christ has been raised from death, as the guarantee that those who sleep in death will also be raised.

In the face of man's greatest enemy, death, there is hope. According to all these Scriptures we have read, the believer will have victory over death.

NEW HOPE IN DAILY LIVING

Not only do we as believers have hope in the future, we have hope in this life. Sometimes eternal life is thought to begin only after death. This is not true. Read the following verse to learn when eternal life begins.

"I am telling you the truth: whoever hears my words and believes in him who sent me has eternal life. He will not be judged, but has already passed from death to life." John 5:24

This verse tells us that eternal life begins when we believe. It continues forever, even after physical death.

Our hope began when we heard the gospel and received Jesus as Savior and Lord. In Colossians 1:23 we read: *You must, of course, continue faithful on a firm and sure foundation and must not allow yourselves to be shaken from the hope you gained when you heard the gospel.*

With the new hope, there is a new quality of the present life.

When a husband and wife are born again, there is hope for a better marriage relationship. A new quality of love enters into that marriage. There are many unhappy marriages in which the husband or wife wastes money and time on alcoholic beverages, gambling, or other immoral worldly pleasures. Often there will be extra sex partners, and there will be little time for the marriage partner and children. This is a picture of a hopeless marriage. But God, in his mercy, loves and allows the couple to hear the Good News of Jesus. They repent of their sin and place their faith in Christ. Hope is born. This family has a new hope.

A businessman lives for money. Prestige, success, and money are his gods. He has no time for the true God. He has little time for his family. Every minute is filled with business. When he wakes and before he sleeps, he thinks only of business and more money. But one day a believer goes to the man's office and talks to him about being born again. The business man, lonely in the successful crowd, tired of running a hopeless race, repents and receives Christ as his new Lord. Hope is born. This hope is greater than anything money can buy.

A young man feels hopeless when addicted to drugs. He has no purpose in living. He is lonely and guilty. He is a black sheep to his family. But God in His mercy still loves him. The young man hears the message of Good News. He believes in Jesus as his Savior and Lord. Hope is born. He is a new person. The old habits are replaced with new ones.

These are examples of new hope that comes when the gospel is heard and Christ is received as Savior and Lord. Therefore, we conclude that there is hope in the believer's life, even on earth. It is well to remember that the secret of this hope is found in God.

In 1 Peter 1:21 we read, *Through him you believe in God, who raised him from death and gave him glory and so your faith and hope are fixed on God.*

So far in this lesson we have learned:

1. The believer can face death with hope.
2. New hope is born in the life of the believer when he receives Christ as Savior and Lord.

NEW HOPE FOR ETERNITY

Now we will study the question faced by every new believer. **After I am born again and then sin, do I lose my salvation?** Is there hope of security for the believer?

In our first lesson we learned that a person sins after he has been born again. Some people believe salvation can be lost when a person sins. But this is not true. If you believe you may lose your salvation at any time, then you have no real hope. Of what value is a religion that is uncertain? Who would be interested in salvation if it can be lost at any time a person sins?

The Bible teaches that when a person is born again, he cannot lose his new life. Analyze for a moment the promise of Jesus in John 5:24:

I am telling you the truth: whoever hears my words and believes in him who sent me has eternal life. He will not be judged, but has already passed from death to life.

40

In this verse there are two requirements to meet before a person has eternal life:

1. Hearing the words of Christ
2. Believing (trusting in Christ as Savior and Lord)

When a person has done these two things, he has eternal life.

What does the word eternal mean? Does it mean temporary? Does it mean until a person sins? No, eternal means forever. A person hears and believes and therefore has eternal life; if this eternal life becomes temporary, then Jesus has lied. Jesus does not lie.

Jesus often used the word eternal or everlasting to describe the new life of the believer. From your Bible, read the following verses: John 3:15-16; John 8:12; John 10:28; 1 John 5:13. As you read, underline the word **eternal**.

When a person is born again, he has eternal life. In John 10:28-30 Jesus said, *"I give them eternal life, and they shall never die. No one can snatch them from me. What my Father has given me is greater than everything, and no one can snatch them away from the Father's care. The Father and I are one."*

In these verses there is a message of security and hope for the believer. Underline the words **eternal**, **life**, **never die**, **no one**.

Let us look at Paul's words on the subject:

Who, then, can separate us from the love of Christ? Can trouble do it, or hardship or persecution or hunger or poverty or danger or death? No, in all these things we have complete victory through him who loved us! For I am certain that nothing can separate us from his love: neither death nor life, neither angels nor other heavenly rulers or powers, neither the present nor the future, neither the world above nor the world below—there is nothing in all creation that will ever be able to separate us from the love of God which is ours through Christ Jesus our Lord. Romans 8:35, 37-39

Please read these verses again and underline key words that give the believer assurance of **eternal** life.

After listing many things that may be experienced by the believer, Paul emphasized that **none of these** can separate the believer from God's indwelling love. In these verses there is a message of security and hope for the believer.

Let us look at the subject in another way. When we were born again, we became a part of God's family. In John 1:12 we read: *Some, however, did receive him and believed in him; so he gave them the right to become God's children.*

As an example, when you were born physically, you became a part of a family. You had a father and mother. If as a young child you were disobedient, does this mean you are no longer the child of your father and mother? No! Good or bad, you remain their child. If you are rebellious, it will hurt your parents and make them sad, but you are still their child, and they are still your parents. If days pass and you are not talking with your parents, does this mean they are no longer your parents? No. The fellowship, the happiness and joy may be missing, but the fact of the relationship continues. It is bad for a child to wrong his parents. It is bad for a believer to sin against God. But if it happens, and it will, God does not disown his children.

Open your Bible to Psalm 51. Read verses 1-13. This is the great confessional prayer of David. In the prayer David confesses his sin to God. In verse 8 David said, *Let me hear the sounds of joy and gladness...* In verse 12 he said, *Give me again the joy that comes from your salvation...*

David had sinned. He confessed his sin to God. He did not ask God to give him salvation again but to **restore the joy** of his salvation. David had lost the joy because of sin in his life, but he had not lost his salvation.

From this lesson we conclude that a person needs to be saved (born again) one time only. When you are born again, you receive eternal life and will never be condemned.

The fact that we, as believers, have eternal security does not mean that we have a free license to sin. A true believer will never say, "I am sure I am going to heaven; therefore, I will sin as often as I want." A true believer will not enjoy living in sin. He will feel uncomfortable and guilty. Because God's grace and mercy assures us of **eternal life**, we will desire to live for him.

The believer has hope when facing death.
The believer has hope in daily living.
The believer has hope of eternal life that is secure.

FOR REVIEW AND DISCUSSION

1. The source of hope for the believer is _____.

2. What is the difference between the funerals of an unbeliever and a believer?

3. According to our lesson, what will happen to the believer when Jesus comes back? John 14:1-3

4. What guarantee do we have of being resurrected?
   1 Corinthians 15:12-14, 17-20

5. If you died now, where would you go? _____
   Are you certain? Yes ___ No ___

6. In this lesson some illustrations are given of new hope in this life for those who have received new life from Christ. How did you see new hope come into your life, marriage, or family life when you were born again?

7. Does the believer have hope of certain life in heaven? Yes ___

   No ___

8. Jesus often used one word to describe the new life. It is

   _____. John 10:28

9. If God gives you something for eternity, how long will you have it? _____

10. Eternal means: everlasting ___

    temporary ___

11. David did not lose his salvation. He did lose the _____ of his salvation because of _____ in his life.

12. Read again Romans 8:35, 37-39. What can separate the believer from the love of God?

LESSON 6

NEW RELATIONSHIPS

In this lesson we will study four new relationships which the believer will experience. When a person is born again, there will be a new relationship to:

1. God
2. Family
3. The Christian family, the church
4. The world

A NEW RELATIONSHIP TO GOD

From the Bible we read:

And you also became God's people when you heard the true message, the Good News that brought you salvation. Ephesians 1:13

Some, however, did receive him and believed in him; so he gave them the right to become God's children. John 1:12

It is through faith that all of you are God's sons in union with Christ Jesus. Galatians 3:26

Because of his love God had already decided that through Jesus Christ he would make us his sons—this was his pleasure and purpose. Ephesians 1:5

See how much the Father has loved us! His love is so great that we are called God's children—and so, in fact, we are. 1 John 3:1

At one time you were not God's people, but now you are his people; at one time you did not know God's mercy, but now you have received his mercy. 1 Peter 2:10

When we received Christ as our Savior and Lord, we became **God's children**, his people. Before we were born again, we knew God only in our minds, but a new personal relationship came when we invited God to be Master of every part of our lives.

What does this new relationship to God mean in our lives?

1. It means **we are led daily by the Spirit of a holy and loving God**.

This means that as we allow God's Spirit to guide our lives, he will do it. When there are decisions to make, we talk to God in prayer about them. We ask God to help us know the right decisions. Whether it concerns college, our life vocation, a future marriage partner, or any other big or small matter, God as our Father is interested. He will lead us by his Spirit. This means that he becomes the head of our home, business, recreation, and of all things. He guides; we follow. This makes life much more exciting for the believer.

2. To be children of God means **we are free from fear**.

In Romans 8:15 we read, *For the Spirit that God has given you does not make you slaves and cause you to be afraid.*

As children of God we do not need to be afraid of calamities and crises. As children of God we do not need to be afraid of failure.

3. To be children of God means **we can come personally to God, our Father**.

In Romans 8:15b we read, *The Spirit made you God's children, and by the Spirit's power we cry out to God, "Father! my Father!"*

Ephesians 3:12: *In union with Christ and through our faith in him, we have the boldness to go into God's presence with all confidence.*

This is the privilege of God's chosen people, his children. God becomes more than just a word or someone far away. He is our Father, present and all powerful.

4. To be children of God means **we have a guarantee of victory**.

In Romans 8:16-17, 28 we read: *God's Spirit joins himself to our spirits to declare that we are God's children. Since we are his children, we will possess the blessings he keeps for his people... We know that in all things God works for good with those who love him, those whom he has called according to his purpose.*

Please read Romans 8:16-17, 28 above again.

The first and greatest relationship for the believer is this Father-child relationship.

A NEW RELATIONSHIP TO FAMILY

If you are the only one in your family who has been born again, you may have some difficult times. If a teenager is born again and his parents have not been born again, sometimes the parents will not understand. They often will not appreciate the "new religion" embraced by the son or daughter. Sometimes a teenager is given a choice of either giving up the new religion or his home. There may

48

be conflict when one marriage partner is born again and the other is not. Jesus warned of conflict in the new relationship within the family.

In Matthew 10:34-37 we read the words of Jesus: *"Do not think that I have come to bring peace to the world. No, I did not come to bring peace, but a sword. I came to set sons against their fathers, daughters against their mothers, daughters-in-law against their mothers-in-law; a man's worst enemies will be the members of his own family. Whoever loves his father or mother more than me is not fit to be my disciple; whoever loves his son or daughter more than me is not fit to be my disciple."*

In these verses Jesus is saying that inevitable conflict will come in many families when some members decide to follow Jesus and the others decide not to. Jesus is not the divider of family members; those who refuse to follow him are the ones responsible for division. If all follow Jesus, there will not be this division or conflict between family members.

When divisions do come and family members do not understand the newly born-again member of the family, what does the new believer do?

1. Understand that though other family members are unhappy, you can be happy in your stand for Christ.

Happy are those who are persecuted because they do what God requires; the Kingdom of heaven belongs to them! Happy are you when people insult you and persecute you and tell all kinds of evil lies against you because you are my followers. Be happy and glad, for a great reward is kept for you in heaven. Matthew 5:10-12

2. Understand that persecution is predicted. Jesus said, *If they persecuted me, they will persecute you too.* John 15:20b

3. When you are persecuted, love in return instead of fighting back. Paul said, *Ask God to bless those who persecute you—yes, ask him to bless, not to curse.* Romans 12:14

4. With patience and persistence, pray for the unbelievers in the family. Jesus said, *...love your enemies and pray for those who persecute you.* Matthew 5:44

Some who are born again will experience a new family relationship filled with joy. It is a joyous day for born-again parents when their child is also born again. There is a sense of fulfillment and completion when all the family is headed toward heaven, never to be separated.

A NEW RELATIONSHIP TO THE CHRISTIAN FAMILY, THE CHURCH

You Gentiles are not foreigners or strangers any longer; you are now fellow citizens with God's people and members of the family of God. Ephesians 2:19

A believer has a new family, the church. It is natural for the new believer to find a local church that proclaims the Word of God. In the early New Testament days we find that when people received Christ as Savior, they became part of a local group of believers. In Acts 2:41-42 we read about people being added as members of the church in Jerusalem. We read that after Peter preached: *Many of them believed his message and were baptized, and about three thousand people were added to the group that day. They spent their time in learning from the apostles, taking part in the fellowship, and sharing in the fellowship meals and prayers.* Acts 2:41-42

Also in Acts 2:47b we read, *And every day the Lord added to their group those who were being saved.* If you have been saved (born again), you will have a natural desire to fellowship with others who have been born again. This group or fellowship is called the church.

Before a person is born again, he cannot be a member of a New Testament kind of church. Many people have some kind of relationship to a religious organization, but when they are born again they will have a new understanding concerning what a genuine New Testament church is. Many unbelievers have the mistaken idea that salvation will be earned through doing certain church rituals. They are afraid not to attend services lest they not earn enough merits. To these people, association with the church is mostly a form or ritual which is done out of habit or duty and sometimes for sentimental reasons. This activity is unrelated to daily living in the home, business, or recreation. For these people, their religious obligation is over when they attend the services, repeat a meaningless prayer, and drop a token gift into the offering basket.

Everything changes when a person is born again. The believer has a new nature, new attitudes, and new values. He now has a new relationship to the church. There will be a **new**.

1. **Love for the church.** *...Christ loved the church and gave his life for it.* Ephesians 5:25 So will we love the church.

2. **Participation in the church**. From the Bible we read concerning the church:

...they met as a group in the Temple. Acts 2:46

...they all joined together in prayer to God. Acts 4:24

They...began to proclaim God's message with boldness. Acts 4:31b

All the believers continued together in close fellowship and shared their belongings... Acts 2:44

Sometimes a new believer may need to leave his old church if he sees that its teachings are not from the Bible. He should find a Bible teaching church. The believer will have a new and much more meaningful relationship to the church.

A NEW RELATIONSHIP TO THE WORLD

In the past, before we were born again, we had the unbeliever's relationship to the world. Paul described our former relationship to the world when he said, *In the past you were spiritually dead because of your disobedience and sins. At that time you followed the world's evil way; you obeyed the ruler of the spiritual powers in space, the spirit who now controls the people who disobey God.* Ephesians 2:1-2

Concerning his disciples' new relationship to the world, Jesus said in his prayer to God, *I gave them your message, and the world hated them, because they do not belong to the world, just as I do not belong to the world. I do not ask you to take them out of the world, but I ask you to keep them safe from the Evil One. Just as I do not belong to the world, they do not belong to the world. Dedicate them to yourself by means of the truth; your word is truth. I sent them into the world, just as you sent me into the world.* John 17:14-18

From these words of Jesus we learn that:

1. The believer is in the world but does not belong to the world.
2. The Evil One (Satan) is active and powerful in the affairs of the world.
3. Believers in the world must be dedicated to God.
4. Believers have a special commission, a special assignment to accomplish in the world.

The believer's new relationship to the world means the world will hate him. Jesus said, *If the world hates you, just remember that it hated me first.* John 15:18 He explained why the world hates the believer when he said, *If you belonged to the world, then the world would love you as its own. But I chose you from this world, and you do not belong to it; that is why the world hates you.* John 15:19

If the believer does not belong to the world, who does he belong to? Jesus answered this question when he said, *But they will do all this to you because you are mine; for they do not know the one who sent me.* John 15:21

The world may hate and laugh at the believer, but the believer has the responsibility to have compassion and concern for the world. Before his new birth, the believer had the same attitudes and values as the unbeliever, but this all changed when Christ was received as personal Savior and Lord. No longer does the believer have the same attitudes and values and life style as the unbeliever. The believer's new relationship to the world means that he will hate the sin of the world but will have a new love and concern for the people living in sin. This new relationship is seen in Peter's words: *But you are the chosen race, the King's priests, the holy nation, God's own people, chosen to proclaim the wonderful acts of God, who called you out of darkness into his own marvelous light.* 1 Peter 2:9

Because we have been changed, we now have the task of bringing this new life to others. This is our new relationship to the world.

In conclusion, please read I John 3:1-3 and I John 5:1-5 from the Bible.

FOR REVIEW AND DISCUSSION

1. Name four new relationships of the Christian.

2. When a person receives Christ as Savior, he becomes God's
   _____.

3. What does this new relationship as God's children mean in our lives?

4. When a child of unbelieving parents is born again, what new relationship can be expected?

5. How does the new believer deal with the problem of persecution from unbelieving family members? Name four things the believer should do.

6. When you were born again, how did it affect your relationships to your family and friends?

7. How did you view the church before you were born again? How did this view change after you were born again?

8. In this lesson we learned that the believer will have a new _____ for the church and a new _____ in the church.

9. What does the following statement mean? "Believers are in the world but do not belong to the world."

10. What is the believer's new relationship to the world?

A NEW UNDERSTANDING OF BAPTISM

When a person is born again, he finds a new meaning to baptism. Many people traditionally believe that a person becomes a Christian when he is baptized. However, this is not what the Bible teaches. In this lesson we will look closely at what the Bible says about baptism. It is important to approach this study with an open mind to the Bible, God's Word.

DOES BAPTISM WASH AWAY SIN?

No, baptism does not wash away our sins. The Bible says, *In the same manner Christ also was offered in sacrifice once to take away the sins of many.* Hebrews 9:28

Because Jesus Christ did what God wanted him to do, we are all purified from sin by the offering that he made of his own body once and for all ... Christ, however, offered one sacrifice for sins, an offering that is effective forever... Hebrews 10:10,12

Christ himself carried our sins in his body to the cross, so that we might die to sin and live for righteousness. 1 Peter 2:24

For God loved the world so much that he gave his only Son, so that everyone who believes in him may not die but have eternal life. John 3:16

It is clear from these verses that Jesus paid the price for our sins when he died for us and that we are cleansed from sin when we believe in him. These verses teach that Christ's sacrifice was once and forever, never to be repeated again.

Read the following verses to find out how a person becomes God's child and is cleansed from sin.

I am telling you the truth: whoever hears my words and believes in him who sent me has eternal life. He will not be judged, but has already passed from death to life. John 5:24

For we conclude that a person is put right with God only through faith, and not by doing what the Law commands. Romans 3:28

Jesus Christ was baptized. Was he baptized to take away sin? No. The Bible teaches that Christ was without sin. *...there is no sin in him.* 1 John 3:5b

The Bible does not teach that baptism washes away sin.

WHAT DOES THE BIBLE TEACH ABOUT BAPTISM?

Let us look at some examples of people in the Bible who were baptized.

Jesus

From Matthew 3:13-17 we read:

At that time Jesus arrived from Galilee and came to John at the Jordan to be baptized by him. But John tried to make him change his mind. "I ought to be baptized by you," John said, "and yet you have come to me!" But Jesus answered him, "Let it be so for now. For in this way we shall do all that God requires." So John agreed. As soon as Jesus was baptized, he came up out of the water. Then heaven was opened to him, and he saw the Spirit of God coming down like a dove and lighting on him. Then a voice said from heaven, "This is my own dear Son, with whom I am pleased."

From these verses we learn that:

1. Baptism is required for the child of God.
2. Jesus was God's Son before he was baptized.
3. Jesus was baptized to show obedience to the Father, not to wash away sin.
4. Jesus was an adult at the time he was baptized.
5. Jesus was immersed in water.
6. God was pleased with his obedient Son.

The Ethiopian Official

This story is found in Acts 8:26-39. Please read the entire story from your Bible.

Now read again these key verses concerning baptism.

The official asked Philip, "Tell me, of whom is the prophet saying this? Of himself or of someone else?" Then Philip began to speak; starting from this passage of scripture, he told him the Good News about Jesus. As they traveled down the road, they came to a place where there was some water, and the official said, "Here is some water. What is to keep me from being baptized?" Philip said to him, "You may be baptized if you believe with all your heart." "I do," he answered; "I believe that Jesus Christ is the Son of God." The official ordered the carriage to stop, and both Philip and the official went down into the water, and Philip baptized him. When they came up out of the water, the Spirit of the Lord took

Philip away. The official did not see him again, but continued on his way, full of joy. Acts 8:34-39

From these verses we learn that:

1. The Ethiopian official was an adult when he was baptized.
2. He heard the Good News about Jesus; then he confessed that he believed Jesus to be the Son of God; then he was baptized.
3. A person is baptized after he is born again.
4. The official decided personally to trust in Christ and he himself chose to be baptized.
5. He was immersed in water.
6. When he had believed and was baptized, he was full of joy. There is joy in obedience to Christ.

The Jail Guard at Philippi

Read this story from your Bible in Acts 16:25-34.

Note again these verses:

The jailer called for a light, rushed in, and fell trembling at the feet of Paul and Silas. Then he led them out and asked, "Sirs, what must I do to be saved?" They answered, "Believe in the Lord Jesus, and you will be saved—you and your family." Then they preached the word of the Lord to him and to all the others in the house. At that very hour of the night the jailer took them and washed their wounds; and he and all his family were baptized at once. Then he took Paul and Silas up into his house and gave them some food to eat. He and his family were filled with joy, because they now believed in God. Acts 16:29-34

From these verses we learn:

1. The man believed (trusted) in Christ.
2. After he trusted in Christ he was baptized.
3. He was an adult when he was baptized.
4. The man and his family were filled with joy after they were saved (born again) and were baptized.

From these three examples of baptism in the Bible, **four basic truths** are clearly seen:

1. Each person who was baptized decided for himself to be baptized. They understood what they were doing and why they were doing it. (There is no teaching in the Bible about a baby being baptized.)

2. Baptism is always preceded by a life-changing faith in Christ.

3. The new believers were gladly baptized without hesitation. They were not ashamed to follow Christ in baptism.

4. Each one was immersed. They "went down into the water" and "came up out of the water." The New Testament Greek word for baptize means immerse. Nowhere in the New Testament can we find an example of a person being "sprinkled" or "poured." All were immersed.

NEW TESTAMENT BAPTISM IS FOR THOSE WHO HAVE BELIEVED.

In Acts 18:8 we read: *Crispus, who was the leader of the synagogue, believed in the Lord, together with all his family; and many other people in Corinth heard the message, believed, and were baptized.*

In this verse we see that the people first **heard the message**, then they **believed** and were **baptized.** Notice the order. This is the same order as seen in the other New Testament examples of baptism. In the Bible the order is always the same. Baptism **never** comes before believing.

This truth is also seen in Acts 19:4-5:

The baptism of John was for those who turned from their sins; and he told the people of Israel to believe in the one who was coming after him—that is, in Jesus. When they heard this, they were baptized in the name of the Lord Jesus.

In these verses it is clear that baptism is for those who have turned away from sin to place full faith in Jesus as the only Savior.

BAPTISM IN THE EARLY NEW TESTAMENT CHURCH

In Acts 2:41 we read, *Many of them believed his message and were baptized, and about three thousand people were added to the group that day.*

Peter had preached and many believed his message and those who believed were baptized, and they became a part (member) of the group (church) that day.

It is important to see that the order is always the same, believing and then baptism. Also from this verse we learn that church membership is only for those who believe and are baptized.

The last command of Jesus to his disciples is found in Matthew 28:19-20: *Go, then, to all peoples everywhere and make them my disciples: baptize them in the name of the Father, the Son, and the Holy Spirit, and teach them to obey everything I have commanded you. And I will be with you always, to the end of the age.*

In this important command Christ tells his followers first to make people his disciples (believers) then to baptize them.

From all these examples and teachings it is certain that being born again (believing) comes first and is followed by baptism.

We also have learned that baptism does not wash away sins but that forgiveness and cleansing of sins is made possible through the sacrifice of Christ on the cross.

WHY BE BAPTIZED?

1. We need to be baptized because Jesus was baptized and commands that we, too, be baptized.

2. From the examples of baptism in the Bible we learn that baptism is a time of showing the world whose side we are on. It is a time of public identification. It is a public, open testimony that we are disciples of Jesus Christ. We are declaring to the world that we are on his side and will follow him.

Through baptism the believer becomes a part of a local church family. In Acts 2:41 we learned that the believers were baptized and then added to the group. When we are baptized, we identify with and become a part of a church. This is why it is very important that each believer be baptized into a church that preaches and practices Bible truths. A true believer will desire to identify with a New Testament church.

When a believer is baptized, he identifies with **Christ** and a local **church**.

WHY BE IMMERSED?

1. The New Testament Greek meaning of the word baptize is "immerse."

2. It was the only form of baptism in the Bible. Christ was baptized by immersion, as were the other people in the Bible examples given earlier in this lesson.

3. Immersion is the only true picture of the believer's death to sin and his resurrection to new life in Christ.

In Romans 6:4 Paul states, *By our baptism, then, we were buried with him and shared his death, in order that, just as Christ was raised from death by the glorious power of the Father, so also we might live a new life.*

Baptism is not a real burial; it is a symbol or picture of a burial or death. When a person is born again, there is a dying to the old sinful nature. This is pictured in baptism when a person is placed under (immersed in) the water. Baptism is a picture of something that has already happened when the person was born again. When the believer is raised up out of the water, it is a picture of the new life received when he was born again. The new life does not begin with baptism. The believer already has new life and the raising out of the water of baptism is a picture of that new life.

I HAVE RECEIVED CHRIST AS MY SAVIOR AND LORD. WHAT DO I DO NOW?

If you are a part of a group of people who have just been born again, you may want to be baptized as a group and form a new spiritual family called a church. In the next chapter we will study about the New Testament church and how such a group is formed.

If you are not part of such a group, perhaps you live near a Bible teaching church. If not, you should search for such a church and share with the members about when you were born again and that you would like to be baptized.

Some of your friends may laugh at you if you leave a man-made religious tradition in order to follow the Bible, but God will be pleased with you, and you will have joy.

FOR REVIEW AND DISCUSSION

1. From this lesson we learn that our salvation is made possible because of:　sacrifice of Christ ___
　　　　　　　　　　　　　　　　baptism ___

2. A person becomes a child of God through:　baptism ___
　　　　　　　　　　　　　　　　　believing in Jesus ___

3. List four basic truths seen in the Biblical examples of baptism.

4. In Acts 18:8 in this lesson we see the correct order concerning baptism. Give the Biblical order in three words.
　　_____, _____, _____

5. In Acts 2:41 in this lesson we learned that the people **heard**, **believed**, and were **baptized** and _____ to the group.

6. Why should a believer be baptized?

7. The word "baptize" means _____.

8. True Christian baptism must be by:　sprinkling ___
　　　　　　　　　　　　　　　immersion ___

9. When should a person be baptized?

10. When a believer is baptized he identifies with _____ and a local church.

A NEW FAMILY: THE CHURCH

When a mother gives birth to a baby, is this the end of the parents' responsibility? What will happen to the baby if the parents do not care for it, if no family atmosphere is provided? If the baby is totally neglected, it will be malnourished and will not develop a healthy personality. The baby will not mature in a normal way. What does the normal, healthy baby need in order to grow and develop physically, emotionally, and spiritually? Every child needs **food**, **care**, and **love**. The parents are responsible for providing these basic needs of their child. Their baby's needs are best provided in the family atmosphere.

There are some similarities between the newborn baby and the newborn Christian. The new believer must have **spiritual food**, **care**, and **love**. If proper food, care and love are not available, it is very difficult for the new believer to develop as a normal, useful child of God. Sometimes we see people who have been born again but have fallen back into the ways of the old nature and are not active in Christian living. They may live yet remain weak and sickly.

How does the new believer mature? How are these basic needs met?

God has a plan, a way provided to meet these needs of his children. Just as he provided the family to meet the needs of the newborn baby, even so he provided the family, the church, to help meet the needs of the newborn believer.

WHAT IS A CHURCH?

We see the New Testament church in the book of Acts.

Many of them believed his message and were baptized, and about three thousand people were added to the group that day. They spent their time in learning from the apostles, taking part in the fellowship, and sharing in the fellowship meals and prayers. Many miracles and wonders were being done through the apostles, and everyone was filled with awe. All the believers continued together in close fellowship and shared their belongings with one another. They would sell their property and possessions, and distribute the money among all, according to what each one needed. Day after day they met as a group in the Temple, and they had their meals together in their homes, eating with glad and humble hearts, praising God, and enjoying the good will of all the people. And every day the Lord added to their group those who were being saved. Acts 2:41-47

These believers were a spiritual family. They acted like a family. They had a new relationship as brothers and sisters because they were following God, their spiritual Father.

A church is a group of people who have turned from their sins to place full trust in Jesus as Savior and Lord. They are then baptized by immersion. These individuals continue to meet on a regular basis as members of the family of God. They will fellowship in prayer, praise, and Bible study for the definite purpose of glorifying Christ and expanding his Kingdom on earth. This is a church.

In the introduction to his letter to the believers in Thessalonica, Paul said... *To the people of the church in Thessalonica, who belong to God the Father and the Lord Jesus Christ.* 1 Thessalonians 1:1

It is clear the church is a group of people who have committed themselves to God and to each other in fellowship and service. A church is not a building. The church may meet in a building called a chapel or church house, a house of one of the members, or in a public place such as a community building, office, etc. The church that meets in a member's house is a church just as the church that meets in a specially constructed building.

Paul said, *Greetings also to the church that meets in their house.* Romans 16:5 *My host, Gaius, in whose house the church meets, sends his greetings.* Romans 16:23

Jesus is the originator, the head, and the source of life for the church. He said in Matthew 16:18, ...*I will build my church, and not even death will ever be able to overcome it.*

The Bible says the church is like a body with Christ as the head. *Christ existed before all things, and in union with him all things have their proper place. He is the head of his body, the church; he is the source of the body's life.* Colossians 1:17-18

In these verses we see that **Christ** is the **head** of the church. He is the **source** of the body's life. The church is under the Lordship of Christ. ...*as Christ has authority over the church; and Christ is himself the Savior of the church, his body.* Ephesians 5:23

Every member is under the authority of Christ. It is important that the church allow no person or other organization to have absolute control and authority over the lives of the members. Christ alone is worthy of our total and unquestioned allegiance.

WHAT DOES THE CHURCH DO?

Read again Acts 2:41-47. In these verses we see nine basic activities of the believers who made up the church.
1. They believed in Jesus Christ.
2. They were baptized.
3. They were added to the group.
4. They spent their time in learning.
5. They took part in the fellowship.
6. They prayed together.
7. They met regularly as a group to worship.
8. They shared their possessions to meet the needs of each one in the family.
9. They regularly added new believers to the group.

Remember the three basic needs of the newborn baby—food, care, and love. From the nine basic activities of the New Testament church, do you see how the needs of the new believer are met? The church studies God's Word and prays together. This provides spiritual food the new believer needs. They fellowship and worship together. This provides the care a new believer needs. And the new believer experiences love in all these activities.

The church also reaches out to unbelievers and shares God's love with them.

But you are the chosen race, the King's priests, the holy nation, God's own people, chosen to proclaim the wonderful acts of God, who called you out of darkness into his own marvelous light.
1 Peter 2:9

In a following lesson we will discuss more fully the church's activity of reaching out to others.

HOW IS A CHURCH STARTED?

Look again at the nine basic activities of the New Testament church as found in Acts 2:41-47. When a group of believers decides to join together to participate in these activities on a regular basis, a church is ready to be born.

A group becomes a church when believers are baptized and decide they will continue to meet as a Christian family on a regular basis for continued worship, Bible study, fellowship, and sharing the Good News with friends and neighbors.

It is difficult to point to the hour that a group becomes a church. A special ritual or organization meeting is not necessary to bring about the birth of a church. A family spirit of oneness and unity becomes stronger when a group decides to be baptized and to continue as a church.

Let us look at some practical suggestions for getting started in carrying out the basic activities of a church.

1. The group needs to set a time for regular meetings. It was a custom of the New Testament church to meet on Sundays because it was on that day that Christ was resurrected. In addition to Sunday, the church can meet on any day it chooses for prayer meetings, Bible study, and fellowship.

The New Testament churches often met in homes. The meetings were simple and open. Everyone in the group participated. Everybody was somebody. Everybody was a brother because of faith in Christ. The class system was removed when they became a family.

2. The group needs to pray for wisdom in choosing the ones who will lead in the church worship and Bible studies. The entire

group should come together to read and discuss chapters three and four of 1 Timothy.

In the beginning, it is not necessary to have one permanent leader. In some new churches the group knows very quickly who should be the regular leader in Bible study. This may be true of the song leader, also. But for some churches, there will be different ones leading Bible study and singing until regular leaders are chosen. The church members, after much prayer, should be the ones to select whatever leaders are necessary. It is well to remember a phrase, "Everybody is somebody," in the church family. One person should not be permitted to do everything. The members of the body must be active if they are to be healthy. Normally, the person who leads the singing should not be the one to lead the Bible lesson. Every member of the group should be able to pray publicly. Human hierarchies begin when one person does all the praying, singing, and preaching.

In choosing leaders, beware of the person who likes to talk all the time. A good talker is not necessarily a good leader. The ability to speak is not the same as the gift of leadership. In selecting leaders, look for **humility, faith,** and **commitment** as the basic characteristics in the leader.

3. What does the church do when it meets? You may want to read Acts 2:41- 47 on page 67 again to see what the New Testament church did.

Each church has its own way of doing things. At the beginning, in a Sunday worship service the group may want to participate in prayer time, sharing of personal experiences, group singing, and Bible study. The Bible study may be in the form of a sermon, or someone may guide the group in a study of a chapter from the Bible.

As the church matures, a normal worship service should have at least five parts: 1. prayer 2. sharing 3. singing 4. giving of tithes and offerings 5. Bible study. These five parts can be in any order the group likes.

Church Finances

After meeting for a few weeks, the church will decide to take voluntary offerings as a regular part of each worship service. The members will become aware that new song books or perhaps additional chairs are needed. All the financial needs of the church should be taken care of from the tithes and offerings of the members. If the church is new and meets in a member's house, it may be wise to begin a special fund to buy land for a chapel. This is a long range project, but it is through the regular tithes and offerings of the members that it is possible.

When the church decides to receive the tithes and offerings as a part of each Sunday's meeting, they should elect a treasurer. The treasurer, like all other teachers and officers, must be a regular, active member of the church—honest, responsible, and able to keep simple records. Usually an assistant treasurer will also be elected. The treasurer and assistant treasurer will open a savings account at a nearby bank. The account will be in the name of the church. The church as a group must decide when and how money is spent. Any withdrawal must have the signature of both the treasurer and assistant treasurer. All expenditures must be approved by the church.

New Members

When there are new believers with changed lives, they are to be baptized and added to the church family. The church family decides who is ready to be baptized. Also the church will decide who will baptize the new believers. Any member of the church may lead in a baptismal service as long as the church gives that person authority to baptize.

We have learned that every believer needs to belong to a Christian family, the church. We have learned that the basic needs of the believer can be met only by being a part of the church family. We have learned what a church is and how it functions in daily life and worship.

FOR REVIEW AND DISCUSSION

1. The three basic needs of a new believer are: _____, _____, and _____.

2. From Acts 2:41-47 we listed nine basic activities of the New Testament church. Which of these relate to the three basic needs? Numbers four and seven relate to food. What numbers relate to caring and love?

3. What is a church?

4. A church is a building. True ____ False ____

5. The New Testament churches often met in _____ of believers. Romans 16:5

6. Who is the head of the church? Pastor ____ Christ ____

7. When does a Bible study group become a church?

8. Who chooses the church leaders?

9. Give three basic characteristics of good leaders.
   _____, _____, _____

10. A normal worship service should have at least five parts. They are: _____, _____, _____, _____, _____.

11. All the financial needs of the church should be taken care of from the _____ of the members.

A NEW REMINDER: THE LORD'S SUPPER

To be spiritually healthy, church members must understand and participate in the Lord's Supper as a regular part of the Christian life. This is basic in the life of the church. In this lesson we will study the Biblical teaching concerning the Lord's Supper.

Before Jesus died on the cross, he called his disciples together to share in a special memorial supper. This is called the Lord's Supper. Sometimes the Lord's Supper is referred to as the Communion Service.

In 1 Corinthians 11:23-29, Paul says,

For I received from the Lord the teaching that I passed on to you: that the Lord Jesus, on the night he was betrayed, took a piece of bread, gave thanks to God, broke it, and said, "This is my body, which is for you. Do this in memory of me." In the same way, after the supper he took the cup and said, "This cup is God's new covenant, sealed with my blood. Whenever you drink it, do so in memory of me." This means that every time you eat this bread and drink from this cup you proclaim the Lord's death until he comes. It follows that if anyone eats the Lord's bread or drinks from his cup in a way that dishonors him, he is guilty of sin against the Lord's body and blood. So then, everyone should examine himself first, and then eat the bread and drink from the cup. For if he does not recognize the meaning of the Lord's body when he eats the bread and drinks from the cup, he brings judgment on himself as he eats and drinks.

WHAT IS THE LORD'S SUPPER?

The Lord's Supper is a memorial. Jesus said, "Do this in memory of me." Every time the believer participates in the Lord's Supper, he is to remember the sacrifice made by Jesus many years ago on the cross. Jesus does not die again each memorial supper. He died once and for all. Concerning the death of Christ, Paul says, *He offered one sacrifice, once and for all, when he offered himself.* Hebrews 7:27b The purpose of the Lord's Supper is to remind us of his death. It is not a reenactment of his death.

There are two elements used in the memorial supper.

1. Bread

The Bible says Jesus took a piece of bread, broke it, and said, *This is my body, which is for you. Do this in memory of me.*
1 Corinthians 11:24

In the supper, does the bread literally become the body of Jesus? No. When Jesus said, "This is my body," he was speaking symbolically just as he was when he said, "I am the gate," in John 10:9 or "I am the way," in John 14:6. The bread does not become Jesus' flesh; rather it symbolizes his broken body.

The secret in understanding the Lord's Supper is found in Jesus' words, "Do this in memory of me." It is a remembrance service. We are to remember the great price Jesus paid when he offered his body to suffer torture and death on the cross. The broken bread reminds us of his crucified body. Our salvation was made possible because of his sacrifice on the cross, and the bread is a symbol of his body.

2. **Cup,** fruit of the vine

The Bible says:...*after the supper he took the cup and said, "This cup is God's new covenant, sealed with my blood. Whenever you drink it, do so in memory of me. "* 1 Corinthians 11:25

The juice is a symbol of the blood of Jesus given on the cross. The juice is not actually blood, nor does it become blood. It is symbolic of his blood. It is to make us remember that Jesus shed his blood for us, that he gave his life for us.

The Lord's Supper is the special memorial service instituted by Jesus Christ. The purpose of the supper is to cause believers to remember the death of Jesus as the source of salvation and the strength of life. The supper is also to remind us that Jesus is coming back again.

WHO MAY PARTAKE OF THE LORD'S SUPPER?

In Luke 22:14-15 we read: *When the hour came, Jesus took his place at the table with the apostles. He said to them, "I have wanted so much to eat this Passover meal with you before I suffer!"*

The first memorial supper was for the disciples of Jesus, men who had been born again and baptized by immersion.

In 1 Corinthians 11:17-33 Paul gave instruction concerning the Lord's Supper. This supper was for the believers at the church in Corinth. Paul says, *So then, my brothers, when you gather together to eat the Lord's Supper...*1 Corinthians 11:33 The supper is for the church. Only believers who have been baptized may partake of the Lord's Supper.

WHEN SHOULD THE CHURCH HAVE THE LORD'S SUPPER?

Jesus said, ...*Whenever you drink it, do so in memory of me."*
1 Corinthians 11:25

Notice the word **whenever** in the above verse. There is no instruction in the Bible concerning how often the church is to have the Lord's Supper. Each church must decide how often. Some say that every week is too often because the service becomes routine and people tend to forget the meaning. Many churches observe the Supper monthly or quarterly. But each church is free to decide when and how often.

WHO SHOULD LEAD IN THE LORD'S SUPPER?

Usually, the worship leader or pastor will lead the service. If the church has no pastor, another member may be chosen by the church to lead the service. No special education degrees or religious titles are necessary for the person who leads the service. The pastor or leader will ask some members to assist him in distributing the juice and the bread among the church members.

CONCLUSION

The Lord's Supper was instituted by Jesus so that his followers would forever be reminded of the great price he paid for their salvation. He wanted his followers to always be reminded that the source of their salvation was his death on the cross. So, the Lord's Supper is a looking back to the cross. It is a looking forward to the second coming of the Living Lord. It is a Supper that should be observed on a regular basis.

FOR REVIEW AND DISCUSSION

1. The Lord's Supper is a _____.

2. We are to remember the _____ of Jesus when we partake of the Lord's Supper.

3. The elements used in the Lord's Supper service are _____ and _____.

4. The bread is a symbol of Jesus' _____.

5. The juice is a symbol of Jesus' _____.

6. Why is the Lord's Supper important to the church?

7. What was your view concerning the Lord's Supper before you studied this lesson?

8. Has your view changed? In what way?

A NEW OPPORTUNITY: TITHING

WHAT IS A TITHE?

The practice of giving tithes and offerings is seen both in the Old Testament and the New Testament.

In Genesis 14:20b we read, *And Abram gave Melchizedek a tenth of all the loot he had recovered.* Abram was a great man of God. God blessed him and used him to establish a great nation. Abram tithed. He had a grandson named Jacob. After a great victory Jacob set up a memorial stone and said, *"This memorial stone which I have set up will be the place where you are worshipped, and I will give you a tenth of everything you give me."* Genesis 28:22

A tithe is ten percent of total income. This is only the beginning standard for the believer. Many believers give more than ten percent to the church.

WHY SHOULD THE BELIEVER TITHE?

1. Because of the nature of God our Father and Jesus our Savior and Lord.

The spirit of giving was born in the heart of God. From the beginning of creation, God has been a giving God. He gave the light, plants, animals, life to man and woman. In the Old Testament days he gave the Jewish nation privileges and responsibilities. He gave the Law to help men live better lives. He finally gave his best, as written in John 3:16: *For God loved the world so much that he gave his only Son, so that everyone who believes in him may not die but have eternal life.*

Because our God is a God who loves and gives, we as his children will naturally desire to follow his example.

Concerning Christian giving Paul said, *...I am trying to find out how real your own love is. You know the grace of our Lord Jesus Christ; rich as he was, he made himself poor for your sake, in order to make you rich by means of his poverty.*
2 Corinthians 8:8-9

2. The believer should tithe because he has received so much.

Paul said: *You are so rich in all you have: in faith, speech, and knowledge, in your eagerness to help and in your love for us. And so we want you to be generous also in this service of love.*
2 Corinthians 8:7

God has blessed us in many ways. We have received eternal life. We have received daily blessings, both material and spiritual. To receive generously and not give generously is ingratitude and selfishness. Tithing is a basic way God has planned for his children to demonstrate their love and appreciation.

3. The believer should tithe because we need a regular reminder that all of our life and possessions belong to God.

The Bible says, *You do not belong to yourselves but to God.*
1 Corinthians 6:19

The world and all that is in it belong to the Lord. Psalm 24:1

"All the silver and gold of the world is mine." ...*The Lord almighty has spoken.* Haggai 2:8-9

All we have belongs to God. When we invited Christ into our lives, we asked him to be our Savior and also to be Lord of all in our lives. This means our house, car, money, cattle, fields, business, etc. are controlled by Christ. Not only ten percent but 100 percent belongs to God. He allows us to use and enjoy his possessions. The weekly or monthly giving of the tithe reminds us that all belongs to God.

This is why Paul says, *Every Sunday each one of you must put aside some money...* 1 Corinthians 16:2 Paul was talking about a regular, every-Sunday offering. We must be reminded regularly that God is God of all our money and possessions. When we believe this, we are careful to seek God's will for how we run our business or use the 90 percent remaining in our possession. God is concerned about the ten percent, but he is also concerned about the wise use of the other 90 percent.

4. The believer should tithe because the Bible says he should.

Note that Paul uses the word **must** in the following verse. *Every Sunday each one of you must put aside some money...1* Corinthians 16:2 In Malachi 3:10 God's Word says, *Bring the full amount of your tithes to the Temple.*

Jesus commands tithing in Matthew 23:23b: *You give to God one tenth even of the seasoning herbs, such as mint, dill, and cumin, but you neglect to obey the really important teachings of the Law, such as justice and mercy and honesty. These you should practice, without neglecting the others.*

82

5. The believer should tithe because this is God's plan to finance the work of the church.

In a chapter on Christian giving Paul says, *For this service you perform not only meets the needs of God's people, but also produces an outpouring of gratitude to God.* 2 Corinthians 9:12

Also in 1 Corinthians 16:2 Paul says, *Every Sunday each of you must put aside some money, in proportion to what he has earned, and save it up, so that there will be no need to collect money when I come.*

In Malachi 3:10 we read, *Bring the full amount of your tithes to the Temple, so that there will be plenty of food there.*

How does a church provide Bibles and song books? Through tithes and offerings of its members.

How does a church provide a building for worship? Through tithes and offerings of its members.

How does a church pay the salary of a part-time or full-time pastor? Through tithes and offerings of its members.

How does a church help sick and needy members? Through tithes and offerings of its members.

A new church, of course, cannot do all of the above immediately. A new church begins where it is and gradually develops needed programs and provides necessary facilities. God will provide the financial ability within the membership when he feels the church is ready and able to use it wisely. Usually a family does not buy land and build a house without long-range planning and preparation. Time, planning, and sacrifice usually are necessary. So it is with some projects of the church.

WHO SHOULD TITHE?

In 2 Corinthians 9:7 Paul says, *Each one of you should give...* In 1 Corinthians 16:2 Paul says, *Every Sunday each of you must put aside some money...*

The answer is clear. **Every** believer is to tithe. At what age does one begin to tithe? When a person is old enough to be born again, he is old enough to tithe. **Every** includes children, youth, and adults. A child must tithe, even if it is from a small weekly allowance. Christian parents should help their children understand and practice tithing. **Every** includes rich, poor, young, and old. No one is too poor to tithe. In Mark 12:41-44 we read about the poor widow who gave all she had. Jesus gave her special praise.

WHEN IS THE TITHE TO BE GIVEN?

In 1 Corinthians 16:2 Paul says that every Sunday is the time to give tithes and offerings. It is wise to follow this practice because it is sometimes easier to give weekly on a regular schedule than to give monthly. The discipline of a regular schedule of giving is needed by most people.

WHERE SHOULD THE TITHE BE GIVEN?

Every time Paul spoke about tithes and offerings, he was speaking to the church. In Malachi we read, *Bring the full amount of your tithes to the Temple.* In our day this would correspond to the church. Since the responsibility for world evangelism has been given to the church, it is reasonable to believe that the financing of programs of outreach should be through the church also. All the tithes and offerings should be given to the local church. Other organizations may be good, but they cannot become a substitute for the church.

In conclusion, read carefully the following verses from the Bible:

"I am the Lord, and I do not change. And so you, the descendants of Jacob, are not yet completely lost. You, like your ancestors before you, have turned away from my laws and have not kept them. Turn back to me, and I will turn to you. But you ask, 'What must we do to turn back to you?' I ask you, is it right for a person to cheat God? Of course not, yet you are cheating me. 'How?' you ask. In the matter of tithes and offerings. A curse is on all of you because the whole nation is cheating me. Bring the full amount of your tithes to the Temple, so that there will be plenty of food there. Put me to the test and you will see that I will open the windows of heaven and pour out on you in abundance all kinds of good things. I will not let insects destroy your crops, and your grapevines will be loaded with grapes. Then the people of all nations will call you happy, because your land will be a good place to live."
Malachi 3:6-12

From these verses we learn:

1. God does not change.
2. The Jewish nation had turned away from God.
3. They were guilty of robbing God.
4. They were under a curse because they were not tithing.
5. We are to give a full tithe to God.
6. God promised blessings to those who tithe.

Remember that the person who plants few seeds will have a small crop; the one who plants many seeds will have a large crop. Each one should give, then, as he has decided, not with regret or out of a sense of duty; for God loves the one who gives gladly. And God is able to give you more than you need, so that you will always have all you need for yourselves and more than enough for every good cause. 2 Corinthians 9:6-8

FOR REVIEW AND DISCUSSION

1. What is a tithe?

2. Give five reasons a believer should tithe.

3. Who should tithe?

4. Where should the tithe be given?

5. Will God bless us if we tithe?

6. Are you going to begin tithing? Yes ___   No ___

   When? _____

LESSON 11

A NEW RESPONSIBILITY

God has a plan to spread the Good News of Jesus Christ throughout the world. **He has chosen the church** as the channel through which the Gospel is to be shared.

Paul speaks about this in Ephesians 3:7-11:

I was made a servant of the gospel by God's special gift, which he gave me through the working of his power. I am less than the least of all God's people; yet God gave me this privilege of taking to the Gentiles the Good News about the infinite riches of Christ, and of making all people see how God's secret plan is to be put into effect. God, who is the Creator of all things, kept his secret hidden through all the past ages in order that at the present time, by means of the church, the angelic rulers and powers in the heavenly world might learn of his wisdom in all its different forms. God did this according to his eternal purpose, which he achieved through Christ Jesus our Lord.

In the above verses underline the following words: gift, privilege, plan, by means of the church, and eternal purpose.

God's plan of spreading the Gospel involves the church. That means we who have enjoyed the privilege of being born again and having a new life also must share in the responsibility which God has given to his people.

Even as Paul received a special gift, every believer receives a **special gift**. In Ephesians 4:7 the Bible says, *Each one of us has received a special gift in proportion to what Christ has given.*

A spiritual gift is a God-given talent or ability. God gives gifts to his children in order that the church might develop into a mature body (family) with the ability to share the Gospel to nearby people and to people around the world.

Concerning these gifts Paul says:

There are different kinds of spiritual gifts, but the same Spirit gives them. There are different ways of serving, but the same Lord is served. There are different abilities to perform service, but the same God gives ability to all for their particular service. The Spirit's presence is shown in some way in each person for the good of all. 1 Corinthians 12:4-7

From these verses about spiritual gifts, we learn:

1. There are different kinds of gifts.
2. All the gifts come from God.
3. Every believer receives a gift.
4. Every gift must be used to build up the entire body, the church.
5. Every gift is to glorify the same Lord Jesus.

Some additional practical truths:

1. **Every believer** in the church is a **minister**. Everyone has received a special ability from God to fulfill a ministry. It is wrong for the church to think of the pastor as "the minister." The pastor is a minister called of God to prepare, or equip, the church members to do various ministries, both within and outside the church body.

Read Ephesians 4:7, 11-12:

Each one of us has received a special gift in proportion to what Christ has given...It was he who "gave gifts to mankind;" he appointed some to be apostles, others to be prophets, others to be evangelists, others to be pastors and teachers. He did this to prepare all God's people for the work of Christian service, in order to build up the body of Christ.

2. The New Testament speaks of various positions in the church, such as pastors and deacons, but the emphasis is on the function or kind of work. Religious titles which elevate and honor a person are not used in the New Testament. Paul was never referred to as Pastor Paul or Reverend Paul. Nor were Peter, James, or John. The most common religious title was "brother" and this word glorified Christ who makes brotherhood possible. Jesus condemned the use of religious titles. So must we. Read Matthew 23:1-12. In a New Testament church, all are brothers, no matter what their gifts and positions are. The highest title of respect we can give each other is brother or sister.

3. There is a variety of gifts and talents but only one Lord, one brotherhood.

In God's plan to spread the gospel to all nations, he knew that a few religious leaders could never accomplish the task. Therefore, his plan involves all believers. Every believer has a gift to be used in the life of the church.

Basic to God's plan of spreading the Good News is **witnessing.**

Every Christian has the responsibility to witness. In 1 Peter 2:9 we read, *But you are a chosen race, the King's priests, the holy nation, God's own people, chosen to proclaim the wonderful acts of God, who called you out of darkness into his own marvelous light.*

In Matthew 28:19-20 Jesus said: *Go, then, to all peoples everywhere and make them my disciples: baptize them in the name of the Father, the Son, and the Holy Spirit, and teach them to obey everything I have commanded you. And I will be with you always, to the end of the age.*

This is our responsibility. To fulfill this responsibility God gives each of us a special gift or ability. In Acts 1:8 Jesus says, *But when the Holy Spirit comes upon you, you will be filled with power, and you will be witnesses for me in Jerusalem, in all of Judea and Samaria, and to the ends of the earth.*

This is our responsibility. We find in the early New Testament church that witnessing was a basic part of the church life. When threatened with imprisonment, Peter and John said, *We cannot stop speaking of what we ourselves have seen and heard.* Acts 4:20 Then in their prayer meeting they prayed, *And now, Lord, take notice of the threats they have made, and allow us, your servants, to speak your message with all boldness. When they had finished praying, the place where they were meeting was shaken. They were all filled with the Holy Spirit and began to proclaim God's message with boldness.* Acts 4:29, 31 Notice the importance of prayer in these verses.

When persecution was strong in Jerusalem, *...the believers who were scattered went everywhere, preaching the message.* Acts 8:4 We note in Acts 8:1, *...All the believers, except the apostles, were scattered throughout the provinces...*

From the **example set by the early church** we learn:

1. Prayer preceded power.
2. Power came from the Holy Spirit.
3. All believers were active in witnessing.

Paul emphasized our responsibility to witness in Romans 10:13-15:

Everyone who calls out to the Lord for help will be saved. But how can they call to him for help if they have not believed? And how can they believe if they have not heard the message? And how can they hear if the message is not proclaimed? And how can the message be proclaimed if the messengers are not sent out? As the scripture says, "How wonderful is the coming of messengers who bring good news!"

Paul also tells of the believer's new responsibility in 2 Corinthians 5:17-18: *When anyone is joined to Christ, he is a new being; the old is gone, the new has come. All this is done by God, who through Christ changed us from enemies into his friends and gave us the task of making others his friends also.*

We conclude that every believer has a basic responsibility to participate in God's plan of proclaiming the Good News to the world. A church not involved in sharing the Good News has no reason to exist.

How can one church be involved in spreading the Gospel to many nations?

One way to do this is through a cooperative effort with other churches. There exists a program of foreign missions outreach whereby churches pool a percentage of their tithes and offerings. This program supports missionaries in more than 100 countries. It involves various kinds of mission work, such as evangelism, church planting, medical and agricultural ministries, Bible distribution, education, etc.

The church can also give their prayer support for worldwide mission work. Prayer is a necessary part of missions. In these ways, even a small church can actually be involved in helping in mission work throughout the world.

How can a church participate in God's plan of taking the Gospel to nearby areas?

When a church member transfers to another location, he can share the Good News in his new home. Perhaps he can begin a new Bible study group which later may become a church. Also, a church can cooperate with other nearby churches in raising finances to send a missionary to another area to share the Good News.

It is possible that every church can fulfill Acts 1:8 (see page 90). Note the verse again. Jesus says his followers are to be witnesses in Jerusalem (home area), in all Judea (home state), and to Samaria (the nation), and to the ends of the earth (the world). Would Jesus give such teachings to his church if it were unreasonable? He knew that every church could begin at home and also reach other nations with the Good News.

We have discussed the gifts that God gives to every believer. We have talked about the new responsibility which God has given to his people. Also we have seen how his people, through the church, can share the Good News with the world. We have seen how believers, through the church, can take the Good News to other areas.

How can we share the Good News with our friends, neighbors, and community?

In Jesus' early ministry he invited Andrew to follow him. The Bible says that after Andrew decided to follow Jesus, *At once he found his brother Simon and told him, "We have found the Messiah." (This word means Christ.) Then he took Simon to Jesus... The next day Jesus decided to go to Galilee. He found Philip and said to him, "Come with me!" ...Philip found Nathanael and told him, "We have found the one whom Moses wrote about in the book of the Law and whom the prophets also wrote about. He is Jesus..."* John 1:41-42a, 43, 45

Immediately after Andrew became a disciple of Jesus, he went to tell his brother the Good News. When Philip learned about Jesus, he wanted to share the Good News with his friend Nathanael.

The believer has a new responsibility to share the Good News about Jesus immediately after being born again. He need not wait to be a member of a special class on how to witness. Sharing good news should be natural and spontaneous. If we receive a special gift, we naturally share the good news with those around us. When we have received Christ and all the blessings of being God's children, we will tell others about this wonderful life. We will share with friends and neighbors about who Jesus really is and what he can do for them. We will tell how we were born again and how our lives have changed. We will tell of the new peace, joy, and purpose that came to our lives the moment we believed. This is witnessing. **Witnessing is** telling what we have personally experienced and know to be true. It is telling how Jesus saved us.

If it can happen to us, it can happen to those around us. The way we were saved is the way others must be saved. The way is the same for all. There must be hearing the Good News and a complete **turning from sin** to place **full faith in Jesus Christ** as personal

Savior and Lord. In witnessing, we tell in detail how we experienced this and how it has changed our lives to this moment.

Some will misinterpret us, some will say we are crazy, some will laugh, but some will listen and be born again, even as we were. Remember the words of Christ as he told his early disciples to go into all the world and share the Good News: *I will be with you always.* Matthew 28:20 To every believer, boys and girls, teenagers and adults, Jesus says, "Go and share and I will be with you." This is our God-given privilege and responsibility. This is the task of the church family and every individual in the family.

When anyone is joined to Christ, he is a new being; the old is gone, the new has come. All this is done by God, who through Christ changed us from enemies into his friends and gave us the task of making others his friends also. 2 Corinthians 5:17-18

FOR REVIEW AND DISCUSSION

1. God has chosen the _____ as the channel through which the Gospel is to be shared with the world.

2. Even as Paul received a spiritual gift, every believer receives a _____ _____.

3. What is a spiritual gift?

4. List five things we have learned about spiritual gifts.

5. According to this lesson, who is a minister? _____

6. From the Bible we learn that a pastor, even as other Christians, should be addressed as: Reverend ___ Brother ___ Check only one.

7. Give one verse from the Bible that says the believer has the responsibility to witness.

8. What three things do we learn from the example set by the early New Testament church?

9. Give an example of how your church can share the Gospel in other nations.

10. How can your church take the Gospel to nearby areas?

11. What does it mean to witness?

12. Name one person you want to witness to.

Bible Study Materials
for Church Growth and Church Planting

I Have Been Born Again, What Next? is part of a system of church growth/planting materials prepared by Charles Brock. The system includes the following books:

1. **Leading a Bible Study by Indirect Methods** is a simple learning exercise of programmed instruction to teach basics about a reproducible, Bible focused style of leadership. Anyone who leads a study of the following Bible study books should first work through this booklet. It will take less than one hour.

2. **Good News for You** is a pre-salvation study. The purpose of these seven lessons based on the Gospel of John is to bring people to an authentic salvation experience.

3. **I Have Been Born Again, What Next?** This book is primarily for new believers, leading them to understand Christian privileges and responsibilities in preparation for becoming responsible church members. It is becoming the choice of many churches for orientation for all new members.

4. **Galatians, from Law to Grace** is a chapter by chapter study of the book of Galatians. It may be used by the leader of a new church or in small group Bible studies. It is written so that a new believer can use it as a guide in the first worship services of a new church. The leader need not have special training to use the material.

5. **John, Behold the Lamb** is a chapter by chapter study of the Gospel of John. It is often used following the study of Galatians.

6. **Romans, The Road to Righteousness,** is a chapter by chapter study of the book of Romans. It usually follows the study of John's Gospel. The leader may use it in small group Bible studies or as a resource for sermon preparation.

7. **Philippians, The Joyous Journey** is a nine-lesson study of Paul's letter to the Philippians. It also is designed to be used in small group Bible studies.

8. **Questions People and Churches Ask** addresses 52 questions most often asked by new believers and new leaders.

9. **Let This Mind Be in You** is a theological foundation book that under girds indigenous church growth/planting. It shows that witnessing is natural for believers.

10. **Principles and Practice of Indigenous Church Planting** is a concise and practical guide for church planting.

11. **Indigenous Church Planting, A Practical Journey** is a comprehensive study of church planting. It gives broad theological foundations and timeless principles as well as great detail in the church planting process.

12. **Indigenous Church Planting In Review** is a handy reference guide for persons who have studied *Indigenous Church Planting, A Practical Journey* and are putting it into practice.

13. **Manual for Volunteers** is a concise booklet that gives vital help to those going on mission trips. The input by missionaries around the world as well as Dr. Jerry Rankin and other leaders at the International Mission Board makes this a must for every person going on a mission trip.